THE BIG GREEN POETRY MACHINE

Green Voices

Edited By Briony Kearney

First published in Great Britain in 2023 by:

Young Writers
Remus House
Coltsfoot Drive
Peterborough
PE2 9BF
Telephone: 01733 890066
Website: www.youngwriters.co.uk

All Rights Reserved
Book Design by Ashley Janson
© Copyright Contributors 2023
Softback ISBN 978-1-80459-591-6

Printed and bound in the UK by BookPrintingUK
Website: www.bookprintinguk.com
YB0544W

FOREWORD

Welcome Reader,

For Young Writers' latest competition The Big Green Poetry Machine, we asked primary school pupils to craft a poem about the world. From nature and environmental issues to exploring their own habitats or those of others around the globe, it provided pupils with the opportunity to share their thoughts and feelings about the world around them.

Here at Young Writers our aim is to encourage creativity in children and to inspire a love of the written word, so it's great to get such an amazing response, with some absolutely fantastic poems. It's important for children to be aware of the world around them and some of the issues we face, but also to celebrate what makes it great! This competition allowed them to express their hopes and fears or simply write about their favourite things. The Big Green Poetry Machine gave them the power of words and the result is a wonderful collection of inspirational and moving poems in a variety of poetic styles.

I'd like to congratulate all the young poets in this anthology; I hope this inspires them to continue with their creative writing.

CONTENTS

Ashton House School, Isleworth

Arjan Johal (6)	1
Adom Osei	2
Anya Hancock (6)	4
James Wingate (6)	5
Paramveer Atwal (7)	6
Abubakr Mussa	7
Aiyla H (6)	8
Alysha Kashap (6)	9

Bromham CofE Primary School, Bromham

Natalie Doehren (8)	10
Raya Willis (10)	11
Lucas Ellis (7)	12
Jenson Grummitt (9)	14
Abbie Doehren (8)	15
Joshua Case (9)	16
Jack Perrin (9)	17
Emilie Welsh (9)	18
Joseph Alston (9)	19
Lily Kaler (9)	20
Freya Gabri (10)	21
Charlie Banks (9)	22
Dylan Bennett (9)	23
Charlotte Stephenson (7)	24
Sienna Fhalora (9)	25
Joshua Millard (9)	26
Gracie Vd Brink	27
Meg Jarvis (9)	28
Violet Davids (8)	29
Santino Ottaviani (10)	30
Sienna Starbuck (9)	31
Emily Bridle (8)	32
Ava Xu-Giles (10)	33
Medina Jaan Hussain (9)	34
Daniel O'Brien (8)	35
Ben Muir (8)	36
Annabel Tyers (10)	37
Esme Jackson-Clarke (8)	38
Harriet Stokes (9)	39
Liliana Bonadies (9)	40
Ivy Atkinson (7)	41
Gracie Cochrane (9)	42
Ellie Clark (10)	43
Milo McKeating (6)	44
Moses Masih (7)	45
Samah Alom (9)	46
Adam Webb (9)	47
Rosie Marie Ingle (9)	48
Stanislaw Chmielewski (9)	49
William Larner (8)	50
Bethany Kidger (9)	51
Alice Fox-Johnson (9)	52
Alexa Thomas (7)	53
Eve Sawford (9)	54
Amelia Lodge-Cammarano (9)	55
Aaron Kinder	56
Jasper Kaya (7)	57
Florence Bavington (7)	58
Olivia Hassard (7)	59
Ava Pixley (10)	60
Henry Brooks (8)	61
Toby Applegate (9)	62
Levi Antwi (6)	63
Freya Little (6)	64
Poppy Chance (8)	65
Max Norman (8)	66
Samuel Dove (9)	67

Lewis Avery (10)	68
Isabel Fitton (9)	69
Amelia Lee (7)	70
Vincent William Ofosu (10)	71
Sophie Kirk (9)	72
Oscar Birks (9)	73
Sam Reeves (9)	74
Mason Comb (9)	75
Amber Freeman (8)	76
Freddie Palombella (8)	77
Eddie Morris (7)	78
Maggie Davies (9)	79
Jack Sawford (7)	80
Mila Cientanni (9)	81

Drapers' Maylands Primary School, Harold Hill

David Vasilache (10)	82
Maisie-Mae Wettner (9)	83

Mossley Primary School, Newtownabbey

Shane Kerr (11)	84
Joshua McKinstry (10)	86
Aaron Bevington (11)	88
Joshua Brown (11)	90
Scarlett McKeown (11)	91
Alfie Brown (10)	92
Joel Simmons (11)	93
Olivia Hunter (10)	94
Eamon Robinson (10)	95
Megan Murphy (11)	96
Sophia Givens (10)	97
Hannah Gray (11)	98
Robert O'Neill (10)	99
Abbie Hunter (11)	100
Henry Thompson (10)	101
Ellie Clements (11)	102
Amiee Morton (11)	103
Emily Boe (11)	104
Patrick Rogers (10)	105
Kacie Smyth (11)	106

Newcastle High School For Girls, Newcastle Upon Tyne

Harriet Davy (11)	107
Tilly Bryce (11)	108
Alana Armstrong (10)	110

St John's Catholic Primary School, Tiverton

Lacey May Grace Radley (11)	111
Darcie Woodman (9)	112
Jakub Skrzypon (9)	114
Darcy Blamey (10)	116
Sophia Cheung (10)	118
Olivier Lopata (9)	120
Lydia Williams (7)	122
Benjamin Dane Greenslade (11)	123
Bethany Williams (10)	124
Lauren Grace Coles (10)	125
Noah Tremlett (9)	126
Lenny Gardiner (8)	127
Oliver Ware (10)	128
Elif Taylor (10)	129
Lily Cumes (9)	130
Beau Green (8)	131
Christopher Pike (10)	132
Charlie Crompton (9)	133
Evie Davis (7)	134
Henry Lawson (8)	135
Max Mcdonald (9)	136
Ruby Perryman (9)	137
JJ Bolton (10)	138
Daisy Greenslade (8)	139
Aiden Joby (8)	140
Ellie Frith (8)	141
Lettie Gardiner (8)	142
Martin William Mc Donald (10)	143
Blaise Martin (8)	144
Albert S (7)	145

The Damara School, Thetford

Talia Didley (9)	146
Shai Simons (8)	147
Bailey Rudd (7)	148

Trinity All Saints CE Primary School, Bingley

Oreva Osia (7)	149
Amelia Farooqi (8)	150
Phoebe Bapty (10)	152
Darcy Mason (11)	153
Theia Blagg (7)	154
Poppy Milsted-Gray (8)	155
Laiba Ali (9)	156
Kacey Firth	157
Violet Ingham (4)	158

Willington School, Wimbledon

Nathan Whooley (9)	159
Ben Cryer (8)	160
Tom Castle (10)	161
Orlando Othoro (10)	162
Christian Stephenson Macharia (7)	163
Sam Bemana (9)	164
Charlie Nailon	165
Fin Pittam (7)	166
Elias Carle-Edgar (9)	167
Marcus Kipps (9)	168
Ben Nestor (7)	169
Henry Uden (7)	170
George Cant (10)	171
Matthew Cox (8)	172
Oscar Cormack (7)	173
Charlie Thomas (7)	174
Thomas Massy (7)	175
William Booth (11)	176

THE POEMS

Rainforest

R ainforests are special because the ginormous trees give us fresh oxygen,
A thletic animals jump between gigantic trees,
I nsects are all around in the humungous forest,
N ature at its finest,
F iery flames destroy the trees,
O verhead, the big canopy shelters the ground of the dark green forest,
R are animals hide in plain sight,
E choes can be heard when a cheeky monkey screams,
S pectacular trees give us oxygen,
T ake better care of our rainforests.

Arjan Johal (6)
Ashton House School, Isleworth

What Am I?

I am grey,
I like to eat grass,
I am scared of mice,
I have a big butt but a little tail,
I am a good swimmer,
I fart a lot,
I have a big foot,
My trunk can drink and spray water,
I cannot go in a boat,
When I run, I feel like I am causing an earthquake,
What am I?

Answer: An elephant

I can't see properly,
I have enormous horns,
I can run faster than you think I can,
I like to eat vegetables,
I am chubby,
My stomps are loud,
I like mud,

What am I?

Answer: A rhino.

Adom Osei
Ashton House School, Isleworth

The Deadly Anaconda

Upon the waters deep and dark,
No one dares to go in the murky Amazon River,
As a deadly, slithery, anaconda lies waiting for her prey,
And watching butterflies flutter past.

No one recognises her
When she blends into the canopy of the trees,
Or the dingy floors of the rainforest.

In the dim ribbon of the sea,
As she watches her home,
She is the Queen of the Water.

Anya Hancock (6)
Ashton House School, Isleworth

Pandas

Pandas and their homes are shrinking in numbers
Because of pollution and deforestation,
We can save their lives.

No littering,
No rubbish,
No smoking in front of them.

Destroying and cutting down bamboo trees
Is bad for their homes and their tummies.

There are tons of animals in danger,
We must protect our world.

James Wingate (6)
Ashton House School, Isleworth

Riddles

I have grey feathers,
I can turn my head around,
I can fly,
I can see in the dark,
I need protection from hunters,
I look really chubby,
What am I?

Answer: An owl

I am fluffy,
I can jump high,
I am small,
Foxes like to eat me,
I eat carrots,
What am I?

Answer: A rabbit.

Paramveer Atwal (7)
Ashton House School, Isleworth

The Arctic

I can see an avalanche coming down a high, frozen waterfall,
I can hear the ice cracking under my feet,
I can taste the frosty ice inside my mouth as it sticks to my tongue,
I can touch snowy, white, furry polar bears while they are having their lunch,
I can smell rotten, pongy, dead fish caught in a shark's stinky mouth.

Abubakr Mussa
Ashton House School, Isleworth

Desert

I can hear a koala bear's soft footsteps climbing up a tree in the distance,
I can see a large, prickly, green cactus,
I can touch the soft sand under my feet as I am walking along the beach,
I can smell the sweet aroma of fallen ripe mangos on the ground,
I can taste the disgusting, yucky, slimy, slippery squid.

Aiyla H (6)
Ashton House School, Isleworth

Ocean

I can hear slimy jellyfish behind me,
I can smell salty seawater,
I can see water and colourful funny clownfish crowding around me,
I can taste a red lobster, which has a shell as hard as a brick,
I can touch a starfish, which is as orange as flames.

Alysha Kashap (6)
Ashton House School, Isleworth

The Wondrous World

S ave all the animals in pain,
A ll creatures to be saved, even ones that eat grain,
V iolent people to reflect on their own,
E verything is important, even a stone,

T he polar bears attract like a rose,
H unting on and off land with their noses,
E verything has a warm soft glow,

P rotect animals from hard snow,
O ver the hills, where all is well,
L onely bears given a home like a hotel,
A nyone and anything to be loved again,
R ude hunters to become kind, loving men,

B ears not to be led near hot charcoal,
E veryone must be respected, even a mole,
A ny plant has its own amazing ways,
R oars for help are only heard on bad days,
S oon our world will be amazing, with blazing colour.

Natalie Doehren (8)
Bromham CofE Primary School, Bromham

Caring Nature

Butterflies fluttering around,
Nature is what we see,
It gives us amazing sights and sounds,
I'm glad the sky is painted blue,
I'm always in awe of the fantastic view,
Why are we so intent on causing pollution?
Surely we should be part of the solution,
It leaves me so frustrated and bitter
When I see so many people discard their litter,
Our planet is withering and decaying,
Let's sort it out now, that's all I'm saying,
I will do my best and do my part,
That will be a positive start,
I want to help preserve this beautiful land,
Which to me is every grain of sand,
We are so lucky to have such lovely sights,
Especially day and night-time lights,
Nature is full of fabulous and wondrous things,
Keep it safe for all that it brings.

Raya Willis (10)
Bromham CofE Primary School, Bromham

Wondrous Wildlife

You think you know it all from Greta,
But when it comes to the environment,
We can all do better.
No one asking you to sit down on the road,
Or stop a coal machine,
But we can have a huge impact
If we all think a little more green.
Perhaps you throw away plastic,
Or your car makes a lot of fumes,
What you don't realise is,
You're sending lots of wildlife to early tombs.
Instead, maybe once a month,
You could take the bus or train,
And ditch the plastics,
So all of us can gain.
Some of us will be able to do more,
And some of us less,
But if we all change one small thing,
We're bound to make progress.

So think about these words,
And what you can do
To improve the environment
For me and you!

Lucas Ellis (7)
Bromham CofE Primary School, Bromham

Our Home

E arth, our planet, our home,
N ature, a place to explore and have adventures,
V olunteering can help bring people together to improve our environment,
I t's time to plant trees and plants to grow our environment,
R ecycling will help reduce waste,
O ils can damage our environment when spilt into our oceans,
N ot time to muck about with the environment, time to help the environment,
M ountains give us water supply,
E nvironment is the world around us, including the land, air, sea,
N oise pollution is not nice for everyone, we all make noise in our daily lives, but we should try to think of others,
T ime to get off the couch and help our environment.

Jenson Grummitt (9)
Bromham CofE Primary School, Bromham

Nature

N ature is wonderful and beautiful in its own way,
A nimals need to live their own lives peacefully,
T he most beautiful sight is the flowers and plants that animals eat,
U se seeds to grow crops and not just kill animals,
R ecreate our world for peaceful times,
U se unique ways to make it better,
A ll around you it is broken, you need to fix it up,
L earn how to make it better and then make it better,

W e need to help the animals, please,
O ur world is changing quickly, so make it stop,
R ecreate our world for love and care,
L ove everything in wildlife,
D isconnect the bad people in our world from our beloved world.

Abbie Doehren (8)
Bromham CofE Primary School, Bromham

The Planet's Plea

This beautiful Earth, what have we done?
It's becoming hotter,
Like the burning sun,
Icebergs starting to melt,
From the Arctic Circle to the Antarctic belt.

This beautiful Earth, what have we done?
The destruction of trees,
Chopped by the ton,
42 million lost every day,
And so many animals
Have died away.

This beautiful Earth, what have we done?
Plastic in the oceans,
Which can't be undone,
100 million marine animals die each year,
When will people see sense,
And grasp the idea?

Time *now* to save our beautiful Earth,
Every human must value its worth.

Joshua Case (9)
Bromham CofE Primary School, Bromham

Our Planet

O h no, my friend's dying, pollution is happening on our planet,
U m, why are humans polluting our planet?
R hinos are being hunted, stop hunting on our planet,

P ollution is going on, help me stop it on our planet,
L iars saying they're not polluting our planet,
A lot of animals are almost extinct on our planet,
N o polluting should be legal on our planet,
E veryone help me stop it by driving less and planting trees and much, much more, to stop pollution on our planet.
T o the moon and back I'll go, to stop pollution on our planet.

Jack Perrin (9)
Bromham CofE Primary School, Bromham

What A Waste

W e need to look after the world we live in,
H ow about turning off lights when you've left the room?
A void using plastic that you just throw away,
T ry and have shorter showers and maybe some smaller baths,

A nyone can help, just by using less paper you'll save some trees,

W ater can be collected in the garden, from the rain,
A ny leftover food can be turned into compost,
S ave old clothes and make them into something new,
T hink: recycle, reduce, reuse,
E ven the littlest things can make a difference!

Emilie Welsh (9)
Bromham CofE Primary School, Bromham

The Ocean

Deep in the ocean blue,
Lies a world for me and you,
To save it from pollution and harm,
I want to raise an ocean alarm.

My family and I call it home,
But it's no longer safe for us to roam,
You've filled our waters full of plastic,
So the action you take now needs to be drastic.

Please reduce, reuse, and recycle,
The rubbish you throw, it's really vital,
If you don't think it's your duty,
We'll both lose this magnificent beauty.

I beg of you, please, before it's too late,
We are all dying at a frightening rate.

Joseph Alston (9)
Bromham CofE Primary School, Bromham

What Am I?

I am a massive marine mammal,
I weigh as much as ten fully-grown men,
I may look cute and cuddly with my fluffy fur,
But watch out!
I am one of the most powerful predators in the world,
I am also faster than Usain Bolt!
I have large feet to help me walk on ice and paddle in the water,
I have small ears which help keep my body heat in,
I may be powerful but I need your help,
The sea ice is melting and I am losing my home,
Without your help, we will not survive,
Fight for us!
Fight climate change!
What am I?

Answer: A polar bear.

Lily Kaler (9)
Bromham CofE Primary School, Bromham

There Is No Planet B

Birds and bees,
Seas and trees,
There is no Planet B.

Don't use cars,
Or even cigars,
There is no Planet B.

Reduce, reuse, recycle,
Plastic use is not vital,
There is no Planet B.

Don't destroy animals' habitats,
It's ruining our planet's format,
There is no Planet B.

By wasting all this energy,
We'll pay the highest penalty,
There is no Planet B.

Galaxies, moons, and stars,
We'll leave our Earth with scars,
So remember, there is no Planet B.

Freya Gabri (10)
Bromham CofE Primary School, Bromham

A Bird's Journey

As I fly across the sky,
The motorway I see,
Queues and queues of traffic,
Polluting the air for me.
As I fly across the sky,
The beach I can see,
A turtle caught in plastic,
Floating in the sea.
As I fly across the sky,
The rainforest I can see,
Trees being cut down,
No place to rest for me.
As I fly across the sky,
The city I can see,
Smoke is everywhere,
Making me feel dizzy.
As I fly across the sky,
The school I can see,
Children picking litter,
To save the planet and me.

Charlie Banks (9)
Bromham CofE Primary School, Bromham

Climate Change

C limate change is making floods,
L ions are suffering,
I n bad places, there's always smoke,
M any plants are dying,
A rctic animals are struggling,
T rees getting cut down,
E nding of animals' lives,

C ats that live in the wild, endangered,
H umans driving cars with fumes,
A nimals in trouble,
N ever again,
G o for a walk, not a drive,
E arth is warming up.

Dylan Bennett (9)
Bromham CofE Primary School, Bromham

Poppy The Perfect Polar Bear

Hey, my name is Poppy and I need your help,
I live on a snowy iceberg with penguins and walruses,
I can hide away and hunt and see where to swim,
But now I am getting very thin.
My ice is melting and we will soon be ice-free,
Please can you do this for me?
Walk more, turn off lights,
It will help me fish at night,
The sun is rising, the sea is warm,
Help me and my cubs keep safe and warm.
Thank you for your help,
Have a nice day, from Poppy.

Charlotte Stephenson (7)
Bromham CofE Primary School, Bromham

Nature

Please help our nature,
You can help by stopping animal abuse,
Please stop letting hot air out of the windows,
You're hurting animals!
Stop global warming,
Stop cutting down trees just for paper,
You're taking oxygen away from us,
From the animals,
But instead of cutting down trees and taking away oxygen,
You can grow trees!
Stop smoking,
I beg you,
Stop polluting and littering,
Recycle if you need,
But if not, reuse.

Sienna Fhalora (9)
Bromham CofE Primary School, Bromham

Nature

N atural plants rule,
A nimals live in harmony,
T rees are mighty and shouldn't get chopped,
U nder the ground, you may see worms,
R espect all Earth's treasures,
E veryone has a responsibility for Earth,

P eople should protect nature,
L end a hand to help everyone,
A lways give passion to plants,
N ever water in the midday sun,
T ell everyone what you learnt today.

Joshua Millard
Bromham CofE Primary School, Bromham

How To Change Nature

The trees are so beautiful,
But now they are struggling to grow,
Because of rubbish left behind,
Oh, I love nature,
But nature is dying,
We have to help it by recycling more,
And help to reduce pollution,
We need to keep our Earth safe,
Plastic can be bad for the Earth,
So we need to reduce the amount of plastic,
If we work together, we can do it,
I know we can,
Take care of nature and the Earth,
So come on, let's save our Earth.

Gracie Vd Brink
Bromham CofE Primary School, Bromham

Planet Earth

P lanet Earth is under pressure,
L ots of animals' homes have been destroyed,
A ll around, we see what we have done,
N ow is the time to act,
E verybody can do their bit
T o stop the world getting destroyed,

E arth needs our help,
A re you gonna change the world?
R ight now is the time to start,
T ime is against us,
H elp the world, it's time to change!

Meg Jarvis (9)
Bromham CofE Primary School, Bromham

Save The World

S ell things you don't need,
A lways be kind to animals,
V egetables, grow your own,
E verybody play their part,

T urn off your lights,
H elp plant trees,
E lectric cars on the world,

W ind energy is sustainable,
O ur world needs help,
R ecycle glass, paper, and plastic,
L isten to the experts,
D on't hurt the world, we only have one.

Violet Davids (8)
Bromham CofE Primary School, Bromham

Plastic In The Ocean

Poor little fishes
Swimming in the sea,
One is stuck in a bit of plastic,
Staring right back at me.
But how did this happen?
I'm on a beach, not a boat,
That fish should be swimming freely,
Not lying here in a plastic coat.
And how did the plastic get there?
Thrown out by people that don't care.
We need to wake up and teach people,
That this just isn't fair.
This is my wish,
For all the fish.

Santino Ottaviani (10)
Bromham CofE Primary School, Bromham

A Bottle's Journey

I am a bottle of Cola on the shelf,
I am purchased and emptied and thrown in the bin,
I am dropped and kicked and thrown around,
And now I find myself on unstable ground,
I twist and turn, bobbing up and down,
Floating in a stream and then through a town,
I'm hot and I'm cold, brittle and broken,
But find myself in a large plastic ocean,
At last, I find myself a home,
With all my friends, a place we now call home.

Sienna Starbuck (9)
Bromham CofE Primary School, Bromham

Environment

E arth needs our assistance,
N ature needs our help,
V ehicles damage our climate,
I want to make a change,
R ecycle and reuse resources,
O ur planet needs saving,
N o more plastic in our seas,
M ountains of waste endangering all the animals,
E lectric cars are better for the environment,
N ow is the time to act,
T rees are being cut down.

Emily Bridle (8)
Bromham CofE Primary School, Bromham

Orangutan

Orang-a-ting a-tong-a-tang,
In branches loose you swing,
Your dreams are full of toss and tross,
And coloured birds that sing.

Banana bound, you reach and fall,
From hand to hand to hand,
You lick and swish and swish and lick,
'Til bellies round expand.

Above a dense, mist-covered root,
Look down on men so small,
Those eyes you recognise as yours,
They can't see you at all!

Ava Xu-Giles (10)
Bromham CofE Primary School, Bromham

We Need To Save Our World

We need to stop pretending
That our world is not ending,

We need to do preparation
To save our future generation,

Recycling is a must,
Or our world will be dust,

We need to stop global warming,
This could be our last warning,

Now we can't litter,
We need to save our Earth, we are not quitters,

Our future generations will struggle,
And that will be trouble.

Medina Jaan Hussain (9)
Bromham CofE Primary School, Bromham

Environment

E arth is in danger,
N o time to delay,
V arious animals are becoming endangered,
I cebergs are melting,
R ainforests are getting chopped down,
O zone layer needs to be protected,
N ow we have to work quickly,
M aking the planet a better place,
E veryone must be eco-friendly,
N o turning away,
T he environment is important to us all.

Daniel O'Brien (8)
Bromham CofE Primary School, Bromham

The Ocean

T he ocean is a beautiful blue planet,
H idden in its depths are great unknowns,
E very sea creature lives together below, including sharks,

O ctopuses live in the ocean and have eight legs,
C olourful coral helps animals camouflage,
E verywhere I can see waves crashing on the sand,
A shark snaps at a seal,
N ot everyone respects the ocean as they should.

Ben Muir (8)
Bromham CofE Primary School, Bromham

Earth's Call

The Earth needs saving,
We're not germs,
People and wildlife are on the verge,
Animals are going extinct,
And people are polluting,
Everyone should listen and think.

Trees are collapsing,
Houses are flooding,
Climate is changing,
And no one is helping,
Seas are filling with pounds of rubbish,
Earth is calling and is falling,
Oxygen levels are falling,
Earth is calling!

Annabel Tyers (10)
Bromham CofE Primary School, Bromham

Protect Earth

P lant trees,
R epair sea levels,
O ur world needs help,
T rees are getting cut down,
E arth is our home,
C areful what you do to it,
T ry your best to help climate change,

E arth needs instant help,
A pologise for what you've done,
R ecycling helps,
T rees help us breathe,
H elp save the planet.

Esme Jackson-Clarke (8)
Bromham CofE Primary School, Bromham

Let's Save The Planet

E ndangered animals
N eed our help,
V ery quickly, and I mean right now!
I gloos are melting,
R ubbish is piling up in the sea,
O ur voices are important to make change,
N ature is in danger!
M other Nature is sad,
E nvironment temperatures are rising,
N ow is the time to act,
T ogether we can change the world.

Harriet Stokes (9)
Bromham CofE Primary School, Bromham

Save The Environment

H elp plant more trees,
E arth needs urgent help,
L ittering is bad for the Earth,
P rotect Earth from pollution,

N ature is getting destroyed,
A s the ice melts, the planet gets warmer,
T rees are losing their lives,
U se more environmentally-friendly products,
R epair ice,
E arth isn't in a right state.

Liliana Bonadies (9)
Bromham CofE Primary School, Bromham

Rubbish

I was flying through the air,
Soaring here and there,
Saddened by the sight of litter,
Thrown without care.

Litter blown into my nest,
This is my home, somewhere to rest,
Crisp packets, sweet wrappers,
Not the floor, the bin is best.

Rubbish makes me feel quite sick,
Plastic bags caught on my chick,
It really has to stop,
Pick it up quick!

Ivy Atkinson (7)
Bromham CofE Primary School, Bromham

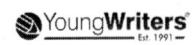

Pollution

P eople are ruining our planet,
O ur future lies in our hands,
L et's reduce waste, recycle, and reuse,
L et nature be,
U se renewable energy sources,
T o make a difference, we all need to take responsibility,
I f we all made just one change,
O ur planet would thank us,
N ow we just need to take action!

Gracie Cochrane (9)
Bromham CofE Primary School, Bromham

Nature

When I watch David Attenborough on the BBC,
It makes me sad to see,
The animals are losing their homes,
They have nowhere to roam,
We need to help the animals and the planet too,
Maybe we could all plant a tree or two,
That's one thing we could start to do,
So please think of the world we have before it goes,
As that would be a tragedy everyone would know.

Ellie Clark (10)
Bromham CofE Primary School, Bromham

The Curses

The stadium of power,
The halls of worries,
The curse of witches,
The power of curses,
The power of swords,
The gods of thunders,
The hands of power,
The avenger of powers,
The storm of lightning,
The fire of dragons,
The rocks of pain,
The race of pirates,
The box of power,
The secrets of sharks,
The opening of storms.

Milo McKeating (6)
Bromham CofE Primary School, Bromham

The Poetry Of Nouns

The dojo of warriors,
The city of stars,
The castle of coral,
The beach of palm,
The stadium of bells,
The hall of craziness,
The house of love,
The field of animals,
The gardens of horror,
The banks of disaster,
The gate of doom,
The cave of peace,
The circus of clowns,
The well of joy,
The river of reflection.

Moses Masih (7)
Bromham CofE Primary School, Bromham

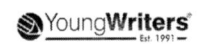

Animals Are In Danger

Lots of animals are in danger,
Their homes are getting destroyed,
This makes me feel bad,
When I see this, I get really sad.

I want to stop this,
It's not good,
Imagine our lives without wood.

If this stops, I will be happy,
Animals will be peaceful,
And will be less unhappy,
This will make me really cheerful.

Samah Alom (9)
Bromham CofE Primary School, Bromham

Love Your Planet

We only get one chance to turn things around,
It's easy when you know how,
Plant more trees and flowers
To give the birds and bees more powers,
Park your car and walk,
So you can enjoy the fresh air and talk,
Recycle your plastics
To become more fantastic,
Don't become a planet destroyer,
Become a Mother Nature enjoyer.

Adam Webb (9)
Bromham CofE Primary School, Bromham

Nature Is Beautiful

Nature is in danger,
We need to help fast,
People should not litter and start recycling,
And with everyone's help,
We can save nature,
We can stop pollution,
With your help,
We can make animals' dreams
To live in a kind world, true,
So please spread this,
And if you do,
The world will become a better place.

Rosie Marie Ingle (9)
Bromham CofE Primary School, Bromham

Nature

Nature is my mother,
She gives me lots of love,
She protects me from dangerous threats,
Gives fresh air, water, and much more love,
Trees, forests, waterfalls are gifts from nature,
It's an absolute treasure that we ignore,
Don't destroy our nature,
Be aware,
Nature is our mother,
It's our duty to protect.

Stanislaw Chmielewski (9)
Bromham CofE Primary School, Bromham

Help The World

O ur responsibility is to use electric cars,
U se what you have, don't always buy new,
R euse, reduce, and recycle,

W hat have we done?
O ur world needs help,
R escue it, it's in danger,
L ook out for wildlife,
D on't cut down trees, that's where they live.

William Larner (8)
Bromham CofE Primary School, Bromham

How I Feel

How I feel when trees are being chopped down,
So sad, I wear a frown,
How I feel when people litter,
Really tingly, a bit bitter,
How I feel when wrappers are found,
Upset, I thought things had finally turned around,
So when you are tucked up in bed,
Children, reunite!
We know we can make the stars shine bright.

Bethany Kidger (9)
Bromham CofE Primary School, Bromham

Save The Earth

Reduce, reuse, recycle,
Get on your bicycle,

Plant seeds for the bees,
Don't chop down trees,
Look after our seas,

Consume less,
Don't get the world in a mess,

Turn off the lights,
Don't take so many flights,
Make our Earth a delight,

We must act now!

Alice Fox-Johnson (9)
Bromham CofE Primary School, Bromham

Little Animals

A cheetah is fast,
If I race it, I'll be last,
I like fluffy cats,
Even if they sleep in hats,
Tigers make a roaring sound,
In the jungle is where they're found,
Bees fly ever so high,
Also, they sleep in cosy hives,
Rabbits jump and play,
A rabbit's foot is lucky, some people say.

Alexa Thomas (7)
Bromham CofE Primary School, Bromham

Polar Bears

I am a polar bear as white as snow,
I am a truly magnificent creature, don't you know?
I live in the Arctic where it is icy and cold,
But now my home is melting, where do I go?
I glide through the water to catch my prey,
But now I have to swim further and further away,
Won't you help me, please?

Eve Sawford (9)
Bromham CofE Primary School, Bromham

Our Environment

N ow more than ever, we need to act quick,
A nimals are suffering along with our environment,
T ime for change, right here, right now,
U nited as one, we can make a difference,
R emember, switch off your lights, get on your bikes,
E ven reuse and recycle too.

Amelia Lodge-Cammarano (9)
Bromham CofE Primary School, Bromham

Rainforest

R ain pitter-pattering,
A lligators chomping,
I guanas clinging,
N ile crocodiles swimming,
F rogs leaping,
O celots prancing,
R ed pandas climbing,
E lectic eels snaking,
S loths sleeping,
T igers padding.

Aaron Kinder
Bromham CofE Primary School, Bromham

Put It In Your Pocket

When you throw litter on the floor,
And a hungry animal comes by,
It could put your rubbish in its jaw,
And then it might just die.

If you put it in your pocket,
And take it home,
Together we can stop it,
Don't make the poor animals cry, put it in your pocket!

Jasper Kaya (7)
Bromham CofE Primary School, Bromham

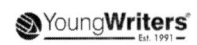

Natural Nature

Green grass,
Blue sky,
Blossom flowers,
Sprouting roots,
Bulbs growing,
Swaying trees in the breeze,
Scrunching leaves beneath your feet,
Look up in the sky, watch the birds flying by,
When you walk in the puddles, they will go *splish, splash, splosh*.

Florence Bavington (7)
Bromham CofE Primary School, Bromham

A Greener World

Do not keep the lights on,
Don't be selfish,
Make the world greener!
Don't drive, walk instead,
Like plants and sow lots of plants,
Make the world greener!
In spring, when the flowers bloom,
Make them bloom forever,
Make the world greener!

Olivia Hassard (7)
Bromham CofE Primary School, Bromham

What Nature Does

The leaves sway,
And the wind whispers,
The grass dances,
And the sun glistens,
The moon shines,
And the stars twinkle,
You jump in muddy puddles,
And you play with sticks,
But this will all stop
If you don't stop littering.

Ava Pixley (10)
Bromham CofE Primary School, Bromham

Litter

L ots of rubbish is dropped on the floor,
I t seems to be more and more,
T he environment needs our help really soon,
T ry to help in the afternoon,
E veryone can do their best,
R eally try, then have a rest.

Henry Brooks (8)
Bromham CofE Primary School, Bromham

Spring

S unny times are coming,
P laytime picnics,
R etro days are over,
I n summer, we will all be happy,
N ations roar across the world for summer to come,
G lobal warming is dangerous, please make it stop.

Toby Applegate (9)
Bromham CofE Primary School, Bromham

Mystery And Problem

Solve the mystery and problem,
It is easy and hard,
If you solve the mystery,
You are finding it,
Which might be different than the others,
If you solve the problem,
You work out the answer,
The answer can be right or wrong.

Levi Antwi (6)
Bromham CofE Primary School, Bromham

Why Do We Recycle?

We can recycle plastic,
We can recycle card,
We can recycle paper,
If we try really hard.

If we save our planet,
We should recycle and reuse,
If you don't want to waste plastic,
We can even recycle shoes!

Freya Little (6)
Bromham CofE Primary School, Bromham

Help The Forest

F or wildlife and insects,
O nly something is happening,
R eally cruel actions are forming,
E verybody, please help to make a difference,
S orry for what we have done,
T ime is ticking...

Poppy Chance (8)
Bromham CofE Primary School, Bromham

Forest

F orests have lots of trees,
O ver the treetops, birds fly,
R ustling bushes dance in the wind,
E astern wind punches the tree trunks,
S top cutting trees,
T ree branches roam the forest.

Max Norman (8)
Bromham CofE Primary School, Bromham

A Perfect Nature Day

Blue sky, fresh air, clear day,
Warm sun, beautiful birds, colourful leaves,
Healthy trees, magical moments happen,
I feel calm, the world feels happiness,
This is a perfect day,
I hope nature can always feel like this.

Samuel Dove (9)
Bromham CofE Primary School, Bromham

Nature Deserves More

N ature needs respect,
A nimals need space to thrive,
T rees and plants need preserving,
U rban districts need containing,
R ural life needs community,
E arth needs human revolution.

Lewis Avery (10)
Bromham CofE Primary School, Bromham

The Seaons

Winter,
Snowflakes spinning,
Atmosphere glistening,
Spring,
Birds tweeting,
Flowers blooming,
Summer,
Children giggling,
Bees buzzing,
Autumn,
Wind whistling,
Leaves falling.

Isabel Fitton (9)
Bromham CofE Primary School, Bromham

Nature

Water clear,
Air fresh,
Flowers pretty,
Dolphins graceful,
Alligators feisty,
Butterflies beautiful,
Trees terrific,
Bees busy,
Nature is everywhere,
So we need to keep it like that.

Amelia Lee (7)
Bromham CofE Primary School, Bromham

Nature

N ice and fresh colours,
A nything is possible with nature,
T rees giving oxygen,
U nited people, help the plants,
R eady to help us,
E verything matters with nature.

Vincent William Ofosu (10)
Bromham CofE Primary School, Bromham

Greta

A kennings poem

Game changer,
Friday protestor,
Passionate speaker,
President meeter,
Boat sailor,
Award winner,
Speech maker,
Book writer,
Youth inspirer,
Nature protector,
Hope giver.

Sophie Kirk (9)
Bromham CofE Primary School, Bromham

Save Nature

Save nature,
Learn to be brave,
Do not cut their stems,
Treat animals with care,
Or your Earth will be blue,
You have a home,
Let them freely roam,
Save nature,
Learn to be brave.

Oscar Birks (9)
Bromham CofE Primary School, Bromham

Nature

N atural world, a mesmerising sight,
A we and wonder everywhere,
T reacherous for some,
U nnatural at times,
R evolving life cycles,
E ternal environment.

Sam Reeves (9)
Bromham CofE Primary School, Bromham

Nature

N ature is
A mazing,
T rees are tall,
U ndergrowth is cool,
R ainforests, we must save,
E njoyment of nature is what I crave.

Mason Comb (9)
Bromham CofE Primary School, Bromham

Help

H ope is here but you need to help,
E veryone needs to stop what they're doing,
L et's all do our part,
P rotect and save the Earth.

Amber Freeman (8)
Bromham CofE Primary School, Bromham

Power Poem

P ower is responsibility,
O ur knowledge is our power,
W ith goodness is power,
E nergy is power,
R ight from wrong.

Freddie Palombella (8)
Bromham CofE Primary School, Bromham

About The Sea

In the water, there are some lovely animals,
For example, a fish,
Here are some tips about the sea,
When you drop some trash,
You kill some animals.

Eddie Morris (7)
Bromham CofE Primary School, Bromham

Plastic

Ocean polluter,
Fish infector,
A useful material,
We need an alternative,
Plant hurter,
Harmful to everything,
Stop plastic waste!

Maggie Davies (9)
Bromham CofE Primary School, Bromham

Green Nature

Green grass, green leaves,
Blue sky all around us,
Green trees, brown branches,
Thin and fat, fantastic sticks,
Nature is everywhere.

Jack Sawford (7)
Bromham CofE Primary School, Bromham

Trees

T rees are good,
R escue them,
E verlasting beauty,
E very day more get cut down,
S ave the trees.

Mila Cientanni (9)
Bromham CofE Primary School, Bromham

The World We Created

The sky is black with smoke,
Cars polluting,
Ice caps melting,
Is this the world we created?

We try hard to stop pollution but people won't listen
Because they think all is fine,
But behind their backs, the Earth is dying,
They don't even care,
Is this the world we created?

In all the smoke around us,
People are too blind to see all of the destruction,
They will never see the true beauty of nature,
Is this the world we created?

David Vasilache (10)
Drapers' Maylands Primary School, Harold Hill

What Should We Do?

Pollution is bad for the planet,
Our home is destroyed by the rubbish,
Look at it now, Look at it then,
Look at what we've done,
Unification, hear my call,
To change our destruction,
I say this is bad,
Only what should we do?
Not only to help us but all things living,
So what should we do? What should we do?

Maisie-Mae Wettner (9)
Drapers' Maylands Primary School, Harold Hill

Pasture Springs

Normally, at the start of spring,
The warm spring air would brush against the squirrel's face,
And the early spring dew
Releases her from her deep slumber.

Instead, this year, the squirrel heard a huge *bang!*
Waking her up instantly,
She then came out of her den in the tree and stared at the once-beautiful Pasture Springs,
Now, a huge array of concrete buildings.

Filled with wonder, the squirrel descended the tree,
As she reached the bottom, her feet touched the ground,
Though it felt familiar, it felt
Different at the same time.

Exploring the new habitat was quite dangerous, weird metal boxes on wheels
Nearly crushing her, but quick reflexes saved her,

The more she looked around, the more depressed she felt,
Animals' homes were destroyed, unearthed, flattened,
Unbearable.

The once-beautiful and lively lake of Pasture Springs,
Now a vat of black sewage, swaying side to side,
Big blobs of rubbish going up and down,
At the side of the lake, where the duck's nest used to be with all of their eggs,
Sadly, the ducklings never even got a chance to get out of their eggs.

Out of hope, the squirrel trudged along to its home in the tree and sat,
Resting its head on its bed of dead grass and straw,
And wished it was winter again.

Shane Kerr (11)
Mossley Primary School, Newtownabbey

The Fox And Pollution

The fox is awake,
Looking, searching for food,
With the polluted skyline of the city,
Always creeping closer, closer, closer.
As she walks past, she sees
Homes of her friends,
Destroyed, upturned, unearthed.
She does not risk a look,
Fearing what she might see.
She runs across the field,
Searching for food,
Thinking of her children,
Getting hungry, hungry, hungrier.
The animals to catch for dinner are gone,
They have been taken to farms.
She could go to the city,
But no, that place is polluted, it is bad.
She decides to sneak in, no one will notice.
The butcher's is in sight,
She could faint from the smell of the city.

She sneaks in,
No one notices as she grabs some chicken from the back storeroom.
She leaves the city and for the first time sees
Really just how little space is left of the forest she knows well.
She runs quickly to her den.
As she arrives, her children come to meet her,
They all have food; they are safe, for now.

Joshua McKinstry (10)
Mossley Primary School, Newtownabbey

Save Our Wonderful Planet

Climate change is hideous,
The ice caps are melting,
The world is warming up and it is serious,
The Arctic is warming up, spine-chilling!

Littering is not cool!
Throwing litter out of your car is bad!
Animals are dying 'cause of this, ghastly,
And people are mad!

Endangered animals are disgraceful,
People hunt and kill animals for sport and money,
All of this is so distasteful!
And so unnecessarily ugly.

Fossil fuels are found underground,
Renewable energy like solar panels are simply great,
Coal and oil pollute the air around,
That is why renewable energy is so great!

Ocean life is dying!
Please stop throwing litter, because you're killing ocean life,
Everyone is sad and crying because the ocean life is dying,
Sewage is rife spreading through the ocean!

Aaron Bevington (11)
Mossley Primary School, Newtownabbey

Recycling Hero

He gets out of his car and slams the door shut,
For now, he is going to walk with a strut,
Over to the recycling bin,
And for the environment, that's a win!
He's like a superhero saving the world,
With his domino mask,
He's choosing no plastic bottles, instead, use a flask.
Now the turtles don't have to choke,
All thanks to that wonderful bloke!
Soon fish won't be trapped in fishing nets,
News like this is as good as it gets!
No sharks wrapped in fishing line,
All thanks to that man, now they're perfectly fine!
Anyone can be a hero, but no one takes on a villain alone.
The choice is yours. You don't have to be fully grown!

Joshua Brown (11)
Mossley Primary School, Newtownabbey

Save Our Planet

E very day the environment gets worse after midday,
N ightfall comes and still it falls,
V alleys carved through the endangered forest, like being hit by cannonballs,
I ndoors is where the animals stay, hiding from the break of day,
R ainfall falls, things are swept away,
O utlook of the deforestation day,
N ow, it is sad to say,
M idday comes and in piles trees lay,
E normous pollution, the forest starts to fray,
N ight workers start to cut and call,
T ime is of the essence, but we have to act, all.

Scarlett McKeown (11)
Mossley Primary School, Newtownabbey

Save Our Planet

P lease stop, this is getting out of hand,
L ove the Earth, it's your truth,
A demand, we should have a stand!
N ow if you want to surf, save the Earth!
E very second counts,
T hink about it and jump off your couch,

E very tree should shine with glee,
A nimals shout, "Please help me!"
R ide the adventure of greatness,
T hen fix up the environment and be gracious,
H owever you think, it's about time you strike!

Alfie Brown (10)
Mossley Primary School, Newtownabbey

Save The Turtles

S ave the turtles,
A ll of them,
V inny, Jr, Jack or Jill,
E very one of them counts,

T he turtles are special to me,
H e or she, because
E very one of them counts,

T urtles are great animals,
U nder or above the water,
R escue them please,
T urtles, turtles, turtles,
L ess and less every day,
E very one of them special, so please,
S ave the turtles.

Joel Simmons (11)
Mossley Primary School, Newtownabbey

The Forest

T he forest is an amazing place,
H elp, please, to win this race,
E veryone help because it can't wait forever!

F orests are losing trees every day,
O h, the animals will not be happy,
R espect our planet and it will be a better place,
E veryone help because I can't wait,
S top, think, and help,
T his a forest, not a bin or Lego you can knock down.

Olivia Hunter (10)
Mossley Primary School, Newtownabbey

Grave Danger

All those animals are scared and in grave danger,
For all they know is not to trust a stranger,
Humans are imposters to them,
They are not prepared for this mayhem!

Sloths, tapirs, jaguars,
Ocelots, kinkajous, lemurs,
Rabbits, raccoons, squirrels,
Chipmunks, and badgers,

In trouble because of us,
Everyone.

Because of the deforestation and pollution,
I think this could become major,
If we do not avoid the grave danger.

Eamon Robinson (10)
Mossley Primary School, Newtownabbey

Litter Life

L eave the water alone,
I t is plastic that is killing sea life,
T he sea is falling apart,
T he animals in the sea are dying,
E nvironment is in a bad way, help it,
R ecycle your plastic,

L ittering is bad, do not do it,
I n our world, we should not litter,
F riendly fish are dying,
E veryone should help!

Megan Murphy (11)
Mossley Primary School, Newtownabbey

Wildlife

W ow! So many endangered animals you see,
I n the land and in the sea,
L iving in fear, for danger is near,
D read some feel, I do not lie!
L ike hedgehogs dear, hiding 'til the coast is clear,
I n the sea, little turtles passing by,
F or we have to act now, it's not too late,
E ventually, they will be 'out of date'.

Sophia Givens (10)
Mossley Primary School, Newtownabbey

Endangered Animals

E lephants are the big animals,
N octurnal badgers are in at night,
D ying turtles are in the water,
A nimals need our help,
N ationwide, be aware of what is happening,
G iraffes are high-risk,
E mperor penguins too,
R hinos are endangered,
E chidnas, small mammals that are endangered,
D olphins are in danger in the sea.

Now. It's time to act. Now.

Hannah Gray (11)
Mossley Primary School, Newtownabbey

Evergreen

P lants are being killed,
L ovely forests long gone,
A long with animals,
N ot as many trees,
E nvironments being ruined,
T ar roads spoil the landscape,

E vergreen trees,
A nimals losing their homes,
R ivers no longer flowing clear as the sky,
T he fish getting stuck in nets,
H abitat loss.

Robert O'Neill (10)
Mossley Primary School, Newtownabbey

Sea Life

Save the sea life!
Save all the animals!
Everyone should help save the environment!
Sea life is eating all sorts of things, like plastic.

Last year, over one trillion plastics got into the sea,
I hope that climate change will stop!
Fish are lowering in population and there are not many left,
Everyone should start to help and get off technology.

Abbie Hunter (11)
Mossley Primary School, Newtownabbey

Tigers

T igers are endangered,
I f you see one, please do not kill it,
G reat are you, if you try and save the tigers!
E ventually, they will be extinct if we don't help them,
R idiculous number of tigers are killed for no reason!
S o many of them used to live in Asia, gone!

Henry Thompson (10)
Mossley Primary School, Newtownabbey

Save The Turtles

T urtles travel through land and sea,
U nder the ocean,
R equire our help to stay alive,
T hey get washed up in the sand,
L iving in the ocean is good for them,
E xcept when humans come and get them,
S omeone, somewhere, save the turtles.

Ellie Clements (11)
Mossley Primary School, Newtownabbey

Take Care Of Nature

N ature is in danger,
A nd we need to save it dearly,
T hink of the animals and insects that live in nature,
U se less plastic or recycle it,
R eady to start helping the world?
E nd ruining the trees and flowers and the grass today!

Amiee Morton (11)
Mossley Primary School, Newtownabbey

The Ocean

Stop, polluting our ocean with plastic,
It is absolutely sick!
We need to do something about it quick,
It is absolutely sick!
All of the sea animals are getting tricked,
It is absolutely sick!
Time is ticking for us to act,
That is a fact!
We can make a huge impact,
That is a fact!

Emily Boe (11)
Mossley Primary School, Newtownabbey

Save Our Planet

Please save our planet,
So we can see the sunset,
Don't let terrible things get in the way,
And if you did good, shout hooray!
Deforestation means losing trees,
Which brings the planet to its knees!
So please, please, please save our planet,
Or everyone will start to panic.

Patrick Rogers (10)
Mossley Primary School, Newtownabbey

Oh World, Oh World

Oh world, oh world, what have we become?
From humans to beasts to killers.
Our littering is murdering this world,
What have we become?
Everywhere you go, anywhere you look, rubbish is there,
Oh world, oh world, what have we become?

Kacie Smyth (11)
Mossley Primary School, Newtownabbey

Global Warming

G rass is the greenest it has been,
L et summer begin,
O nly, this year, there is something different,
B etween the happiness of summer,
A creature lurks over Earth,
L ike a vast shadow,

W e must stop global warming!
A nd help the planet,
R estore the forests,
M ake Earth cooler,
I nstead of warming it,
N atural resources are now scarce,
G lobal warming is the worst!

Harriet Davy (11)
Newcastle High School For Girls, Newcastle Upon Tyne

Our Delicate Trees

Our delicate trees,
Trees are going extinct now,
Oxygen is running low,
Don't chop the trees down,

Our sacred globe,
Reduce waste today,
Recycle old rubbish now,
Reuse your plastic,

Our precious air,
An animal killer,
Pollution is at large now,
Oil and gas kill air,

Our flooding city,
Ice is slowly dying,
Global warming is killing,
Do something about it,

What am I?
I came from the clouds,
If they clash I am born,

I am very hot,
If I strike, fire comes alight,
I don't want to harm you,
What am I?

Answer: Thunder and lightning.

Tilly Bryce (11)
Newcastle High School For Girls, Newcastle Upon Tyne

Forest Fire

It used to be a magnificent place,
The wind singing, the trees smoothly dancing,
But then horror hit, fire,
It walks to murder every unfortunate mortal in its path,
With the consuming devil in it,
Trees fall with a desperate cry,
Animals in fear of the unstoppable, out of control, breathing fire,
Burning their beloved once-beautiful homes in front of their terror-struck eyes!

Alana Armstrong (10)
Newcastle High School For Girls, Newcastle Upon Tyne

Help The Planet

N ature is so beautiful and wonderful,
A ll we need to do is protect it and love it,
T rees are getting burned or chopped down,
U nder the seas, sea creatures are dying,
R ainforests are dying,
E arth needs help!

We need to look after the Earth
Which we have destroyed,
What we once loved
Will be gone,
We need to help the animals,
We are invading their habitats,
The animals God created for us,
We need to love each other,
Why are we ruining God's wonderful plan?
Our only hope to live,
We are God's children,
We need to look after the amazing world
He made for us,
Help us save the world,
So all the innocent living things don't suffer.

Lacey May Grace Radley (11)
St John's Catholic Primary School, Tiverton

Let's Stop Pollution

Try to use a bike, or maybe go on a hike,
Pollution is a huge hurricane.
We need to stop this, but how?

Pollution is a pathway to trouble, but it's all about to double,
Pollution is a smelly gas that is terrible for animals,
It is a huge brown tornado ruining the Earth,
To help the animals, we could build a cave,
It might save them.

Pollution is a mist but it won't blow a kiss,
You might take a risk, but pollution won't miss.

It's important we care for our planet,
This planet has had it,
Try to use any other vehicle,
You're making the animals tearful.

Pollution is poisonous,
Don't use a vehicle with a dirty, dull engine,
Use a bright blue bike instead,
Pollution is a brown balloon,

So don't use a car,
Life isn't a light, you don't live forever.

Imagine this being you,
A big brown mist blowing in the air,
Then coming down, bouncing everywhere,
Pollution is brown water vapour.

Darcie Woodman (9)
St John's Catholic Primary School, Tiverton

Save Our Earth

There's a lot of green but people are mean,
Trees sway and say,
"Stop cutting us down, we provide fresh oxygen."
Rain drops and stops,
But still provides water,
Rabbits squeak while nature sleeps,
Never destroy this fantastic world,
At the seas, they shriek,
"The water is getting polluted."
The world is near extinction,
Unify the Earth,
Reconsider your actions on the Earth,
End the pollution,
May the world live in peace,
Birds fly, dogs bark, cats miaow,
Ah, all of this beauty is nature!
So we need to take care of it,
The wonder of nature, the fresh smell of the air.
We love this and we live on it,
The flowers swing around like kids at a park,
Leaves fall, this is wonderful,

Everything we have got, we need to take care of,
It's not unlimited, it ends,
So this beautiful nature has to be respected.

Jakub Skrzypon (9)
St John's Catholic Primary School, Tiverton

Destroyed

We need to change,
We destroyed the centre of life,
We destroyed all that's valuable,
Once was the Amazon forest,
Now Amazon desert,
For the Earth is not renewable,
If it was, we would have renewed by now,
Trees and seas scream,
Destroyed, everything destroyed,
Why did we kill what we loved?
Oceans are warming,
Is this global warming?
What did we do to the Earth?
We need to bring the Earth back with a flick of a switch,
Sorry, I wish it was that easy,
Turn off the lights,
Pick up your rubbish,
Don't put things in the sea,

The end is near,
Our home is dead,
Trees gone,
Seas polluted,
Why are we this way?
We are killing what we live on,
Our planet,
Earth,
Why have we become hostile to this place?
Trees gasp for air,
The sky waves away smoke,
We are going to have no home,
I hope you're sorry.
I hope together we can build a better future out of what we have left.

Darcy Blamey (10)
St John's Catholic Primary School, Tiverton

The Four Elements

The four elements are so wonderful,
Fire, earth, wind and water,
They're just so special and powerful,
And so helpful for us.

Fire keeps us warm,
Fire is lovely,
We can toast marshmallows,
Which are really yummy.

Water is the best,
Water is lovely,
It helps us stay hydrated,
And it's very refreshing.

Earth is calming,
Earth is peaceful,
Lots of things are green,
And the rest is just berries.

Wind is cooling,
Wind is peaceful,
It gives us a little breeze,
And it feels lovely.

The four elements are so wonderful,
Fire, earth, wind and water,
They're just so special and powerful,
And so helpful for us.

Sophia Cheung (10)
St John's Catholic Primary School, Tiverton

Help The Earth

The Earth,
Our home, everyone's home,
And it's in danger and needs urgent help,
If the Earth could talk it'd say,
"Help me, the humans are destroying their only home."

All the factories, all the polluting power plants,
Polluting the Earth and making species die out,
All the plastic, all the rubbish,
Causing the Earth to be filled with trash and killing sea animals,
We have to make a change.

Placing solar panels, not cutting down trees,
Windmills and nuclear power reactors,
They don't harm the Earth,
Or harm anything or anyone,
All safe for everyone.

Picking up plastic, picking up litter,
Saving energy, saving power,
Helping the people helps the Earth
Helps everyone to live in a harmless, safe world.

Olivier Lopata (9)
St John's Catholic Primary School, Tiverton

Amazing Animals

A wesome pink candyfloss flamingos,
M agnificent owl hooting in the night,
A ir-breathing crocodiles emerging everywhere,
Z ingy zebras everywhere to see,
I nteresting sharks stare everywhere,
N octurnal badgers in holes of mud,
G arden-green caterpillars live on the leaf,

A dorable puppies in the grass,
N ature lives everywhere,
I magine giraffes eating leaves at every height,
M agnetic snails slide in every direction,
A n enormous bear jumps on the spot,
L ions groom their manes on a thick branch,
S nakes slither across the leaves.

Lydia Williams (7)
St John's Catholic Primary School, Tiverton

The Hurt Earth

The Earth is our home,
Its atmosphere is like a dome over our heads,
It is also home to many other creatures,
But the world is dying because of us,
The ice caps are warming and melting,
When we dig holes to find oil and burn it,
Summer's reached high temperatures,
As you can see, our Earth is being messed up,
Creatures' homes are being taken,
Just so we can have bacon,
Well, I say it's wrong, we need to find a balance,
Or if we don't, our world will die with us,
Deforestation is killing oxygen producers,
The fish are being overcaught,
To be bought by us in a shop,
People all over the world are protesting,
Many of them now live where forests once were.

Benjamin Dane Greenslade (11)
St John's Catholic Primary School, Tiverton

Disaster

Skiing through the Arctic,
I can feel the melted snow beneath my feet,
I can hear the cry of polar bear cubs floating out to sea,
I can see the blazing sun thawing the ice below.

Running in the rainforest,
I can hear the sound of crackling trees,
I can feel the heat of the burning wildfire,
I can smell the smouldering leaves and bushes.

Swimming in the sea,
I can see sea creatures trapped in plastic,
I can feel rubbish between my toes,
I can smell polluted air surrounding me.

Roaming through the wood,
I can hear the sound of trees crashing down on the forest floor,
I can see tree stumps with no trees,
I feel guilty.

Please help our world, a disaster is coming.

Bethany Williams (10)
St John's Catholic Primary School, Tiverton

All About Nature

Lots of different animals are in danger,
And we are destroying their homes,
We have to stop.

This is the animals' world too,
We cannot destroy it,
God made this world for all of us,
So we have to share it.

Animal, butterfly,
All so preciously pretty,
Snoozing sloth,
Oh so sleepy, can't get enough.

The world is not a rubbish bin,
We need to stop littering,
Put it in the bin.

The world is like a bomb, shooting down to Earth,
We have to stop all the wars we do,
Killing all the animals for skin is cruel,
God made us to be kind, not cruel.

Lauren Grace Coles (10)
St John's Catholic Primary School, Tiverton

Pollution

The rubbish being dropped on the ground,
Being blown to the sea by the wind,
Killing sea animals and even birds,
We have to help the animals,
Put the rubbish in the bin.

Some sea animals are going extinct,
People are dropping horrible rubbish on the ground,
It is going around the animals' heads, so all the animals are dying,
Take the rubbish off the animals.

Trees are giraffes giving us oxygen,
Flowers are butterflies with beautiful wings,
Glaciers are frozen turtles swimming through the sea,
The sea is a giant glass of water,
The sky is a dragon flying in circles.

Noah Tremlett (9)
St John's Catholic Primary School, Tiverton

Amazing Animals

A wesome grey cats miaowing,
M ighty, strong pumas sneaking through the jungle,
A mazing, caring, small mice,
Z ebras running through the grass,
I ncredible, big, mighty tigers growling,
N ice, friendly, lazy dogs waiting for food,
G littery, pink candyfloss flamingos,

A mazing flappy fish waiting for food,
N aughty, lazy, cheeky, gorillas,
I ncredible, strong bald eagle,
M ighty, strong lions growling,
A wesome, caring, beautiful cows,
L azy or not lazy animals are living in the world.

Lenny Gardiner (8)
St John's Catholic Primary School, Tiverton

Saving The Earth

Animals are smart species,
They help the world grow,
But hunters are killing these majestic breeds,
So we need to stop this by eating some vegetables,
Stop cutting down trees because animals live in these habitats,
However, we don't just need trees for animals,
We also need them for oxygen,
We need to stop killing the trees,
We have them for a reason, especially sloths,
They bring us bright, beautiful land,
So stop chopping them down,
So they can start using the trees that are healthy for sloths,
And that is the end of my poem about the Earth.

Oliver Ware (10)
St John's Catholic Primary School, Tiverton

Save Our Earth

In the Arctic, the sun is shining,
Icebergs melting, polar bears dying,
Your poor Mother Earth is weeping and crying.

Hungry families, crops suffering from drought,
Your people and creatures dying all about,
We need to save our Earth before it all expires out.

Your land seems to be turning to waste,
Your animals think it has an appetising taste,
To find it's like a disgusting-tasting paste,

Please save this world that we were set to protect,
It seems everyone has started to forget how our
Earth needs us to stop harming it,
So today, please save our planet!

Elif Taylor (10)
St John's Catholic Primary School, Tiverton

Nature

Nature is a massive, magical place
That gets your head thinking,
What should I do outside next?
How should I climb this tree?

Animals are losing their homes because of us,
We have to stop cutting down trees,
Birds, koalas, pandas, sloths, squirrels,
And many more animals are losing homes.

Trees are gigantic broccoli,
They are huge skyscrapers,
They are tiny mice.

Foxes are red fluffy bushes,
Cats are bendy branches,
Dogs are furry potatoes,
Rabbits are bouncy frogs.

Lily Cumes (9)
St John's Catholic Primary School, Tiverton

Sea

Sea creatures are endangered because there is rubbish everywhere,
All that rubbish should be thrown away with care,
Instead, the rubbish is a massive moving mountain floating menacingly across the sea,
The rubbish is a black hole crushing creatures and their homes,

All the rubbish going into the sea,
Some of the creatures are dying, they shouldn't be,
We need to stop throwing our rubbish everywhere,
All that rubbish should be thrown away with care.

Beau Green (8)
St John's Catholic Primary School, Tiverton

Nature

Nature is everywhere and we all should take care of it,
Nature is damaged and trees chopped down,
Nature is the future of a desolate desert land,
Nature is the land swept away by a wave that destroys,

Nature is the rainforest, a beautiful breeze blowing birds through the branches,
Nature is the oceans calmly flowing past,
Nature is the future if people take care,
Nature is everywhere and we should all take care of it.

Christopher Pike (10)
St John's Catholic Primary School, Tiverton

Sea

The sea is full of rubbish that shouldn't be there,
Sea creatures get trapped and suffer because we don't care,
The rubbish is a spider, spinning its endless web,
Trapping its prey under its floating bed,

The sea gives us the food that we need,
The sea gives us the air that we breathe,
The sea must not be full of rubbish that shouldn't be there,
Sea creatures must not suffer, and we need to care.

Charlie Crompton (9)
St John's Catholic Primary School, Tiverton

Our Planet

I love the fresh air that flows in our bodies,
I love the feel of the soft green grass on our planet,
I love the smell of gooey cookies baking in the oven,
I love the fierce tigers hunting around, trying to live their amazing lives,
I love the smell of candy because it's an amazing smell,
I love the polar bears, fierce and brave, ready to pounce at their prey,
I love the sound of the crashing waves.

Evie Davis (7)
St John's Catholic Primary School, Tiverton

The Glacier

The glacier is a river of ice in the cold, dark sea,
Crying as it melts through the colossal, icy sea.

The glacier is a racing river of ice,
Dissolving in the salty, shimmering sea.

The glacier is a plain piece of paper,
All scrunched up and thrown away,
Shrinking in the icy, gloomy sea.

The glacier is a gigantic block of ice,
Evaporating into the misty, mysterious sea.

Henry Lawson (8)
St John's Catholic Primary School, Tiverton

Endangered Animals

Tall trees are butterflies gliding through the wonderful fresh air,
Poachers are cheetahs hunting animals and attacking anything they can sell part of,
Pandas and penguins are bees after they sting, slowly going extinct,
Trees are rockets slowly leaving the Earth, but they give us oxygen, we need to stop deforestation,
Poachers are fierce lions attacking and murdering mercilessly for nothing but money.

Max Mcdonald (9)
St John's Catholic Primary School, Tiverton

Wildlife

The rainforest is full of beautiful wildlife and amazing animals,
Why are we cutting down trees?
Animals are lost before they are found,
Greedy people taking more than they should,

The rainforest is a hibernating bear, curled up carefully in a cosy cave,
Why are we taking more than we need?
We need to take care of all that we have,
And let the bear sleep peacefully from harm.

Ruby Perryman (9)
St John's Catholic Primary School, Tiverton

Our Earth

When we wake, we hurt the Earth,
When we drop trash on the ground,
The Earth is weakened, 'til one day,
The Earth will be broken from what we have done,
No one but us can save the world,
And the people in it,
We can stop world hunger,
Because God won't, so we will,
So let's make the Earth a better place.

JJ Bolton (10)
St John's Catholic Primary School, Tiverton

What Am I?

I am a blur of black and white soaring through the ocean,
I waddle through the Arctic as slow as a tortoise,
My egg is always toasty in the fluff underneath my legs,
I leave the egg with the dad to go fishing,
My baby cannot swim when it's born,
I get eaten by killer whales,
What am I?

Daisy Greenslade (8)
St John's Catholic Primary School, Tiverton

Our Planet

I love listening to the birds tweeting,
I love hearing the breezy wind blow,
I love smelling the fresh air,

- **E** xcellent animals playing,
- **A** mazing places to go,
- **R** efreshing fresh air,
- **T** he beautiful plants growing,
- **H** earing lots of people chatting.

Aiden Joby (8)
St John's Catholic Primary School, Tiverton

Earth

I love the Earth and windy days,
I love the kind creatures on Earth,
I love how the world can be a mystery,
I love all the kind people,
I love all the nice houses,
I love all the food that people make for us,
I love all the people that take care of us.

Ellie Frith (8)
St John's Catholic Primary School, Tiverton

What Kind Of Magic Can The Puppy Do?

I can do card tricks and really good magical skills like creating masks,
I can do fire tricks and water magic,
I can do really good fire magic and really cool wind magic,
I can do some animal magic,
Finally, my best magic is finding any pet that needs help.

Lettie Gardiner (8)
St John's Catholic Primary School, Tiverton

Nature So Clean

Take a closer look at nature,
At the birds and the bees,
The beauty that lives in nature,
Beauty might go,
And the polar snow,
Why? you say,
The axes are swinging,
And now the tree creatures are in pain,
But we can make a change,
So be nicer to nature, so clean.

Martin William Mc Donald (10)
St John's Catholic Primary School, Tiverton

Our World Needs Saving

Stop throwing rubbish into the sea,
Don't chop nature's trees down,
Stop hurting endangered animals,
Stop the pollution,
Stop the littering,
Stop destroying our lovely planet,
Protect our lovely species from danger.

Blaise Martin (8)
St John's Catholic Primary School, Tiverton

What Am I?

I love the white fur and the black spots,
And how fast it goes,
Also, how it gets its prey,
I love how it runs,
And how it smells its prey,
I like how it eats its prey,
I like its sharp teeth.

Albert S (7)
St John's Catholic Primary School, Tiverton

Earth

Earth gave us clean water,
We made the water dirty,
Earth gave us good animals,
We abused the animals,
Earth gave us healthy air,
We made pollution in the air,
Earth gave us healthy forests,
We cut trees for money,
Earth gave us healthy flowers,
We ruined the flowers,
Earth gave us nice rhinos
We wanted their horns,
Earth made everything pretty,
We made it look worse,
Earth did nothing wrong,
Save the world!

Talia Didley (9)
The Damara School, Thetford

Nature Corrupted

Help save the world and nature,
People litter every day, it kills us,
Humans destroy habitats and the ocean,
Throw rubbish in the bin.

Save the world by throwing rubbish in the bin,
Littering is bad, throw rubbish in the bin and help nature,
Throw rubbish in the bin, lots of people get away with it,
Throw rubbish in the bin, an animal dies every day,
Throw rubbish in the bin and keep the world safe.

Shai Simons (8)
The Damara School, Thetford

Rubbish, Rubbish Everywhere

Rubbish, rubbish everywhere,
It seems that people just don't care,
Now we need to clean it up,
Get our friends to pick it up,
Keep our planet nice and clean,
Now we need to eat some beans,
Now it's time to go and clean,
Keep our planet nice and green!

Bailey Rudd (7)
The Damara School, Thetford

Helping Nature

Saving nature is a hard thing to do,
Because you have to pick up trash
From the ground,
And the trees will dry out,
And the waters will be dirty,
You have to do a lot of things
To make Earth a better place,
Cleaning Earth is important
Because millions of humans and animals
Have died because of toxic waste,
And plastic being on the ground,
That is why all of us need to
Make Earth a better place.

Oreva Osia (7)
Trinity All Saints CE Primary School, Bingley

Save Our Planet!

Trees, trees,
In the forest,
Getting destroyed,
Pretty sad, to be honest.

Bees, bees,
Buzzing around,
No pollen to eat,
Now no bees to be found.

Bears, bears,
We've melted your home,
No food for your stomach,
No place for you to roam.

Earth, Earth,
We will consume,
We will destroy,
We will be doomed.

Please, please,
Spread the word,
Save our planet,
Save our world.

Amelia Farooqi (8)
Trinity All Saints CE Primary School, Bingley

Save Our World

There's lots of plastic in the sea,
To save animals, we must be,
Working in motion,
To save our ocean,
Who can do that?
Oh, I know, me!

Climate change, it's not much better,
To help us, let's ask our friend Greta,
"Campaign for what's right,
Then Earth's future is bright."
Follow her lead, don't upset her.

Phoebe Bapty (10)
Trinity All Saints CE Primary School, Bingley

Rainforest Life!

Rainforests are peaceful and happy places,
Just as animals love to live,
Animals are extinct because of the fires,
Trees are cut down so there's no oxygen left.

Littering is a danger to this world,
Like animals are dying, as you know,
So please save our animals and trees today,
As you know, we live today.

Darcy Mason (11)
Trinity All Saints CE Primary School, Bingley

Animal Lover Dove

When you sleep, the animal lover dove
Comes into your dreams,
Cats, dogs, foxes, and hedgehogs,
Sparkling and dancing in the night,
When midnight strikes,
The mouse will go in,
Then they will go,
Leaving the animal lover dove alone,
Disappearing into the air.

Theia Blagg (7)
Trinity All Saints CE Primary School, Bingley

Sunflower

S unshine,
U p to the sky,
N ormally found in sunny places,
F riendly,
L ovely,
O ver our heads,
W onderful,
E xtremely tall,
R ough leaves.

Poppy Milsted-Gray (8)
Trinity All Saints CE Primary School, Bingley

The World

W orld is so green,
O lder are loving the breath of fresh air,
R eminiscing about summers abroad,
L oving living life to the max,
D reaming of the blessings of every day.

Laiba Ali (9)
Trinity All Saints CE Primary School, Bingley

Nature

Flowers and leaves,
Wildlife and trees,
Sounds so good to me.

Butterflies fly,
Frogs go *splash*,
Come on, let's make some mash!

Kacey Firth
Trinity All Saints CE Primary School, Bingley

The Earth

The Earth is big,
It is our planet,
It is our job
To try and save it!

Violet Ingham (4)
Trinity All Saints CE Primary School, Bingley

Eco-Friendly

E co committees help the world all the time by recycling and reusing,
C an you do anything to help the world as well?
O h yes, you can - how about turning vegan?

F or the next generation to come,
R ecycle instead of throwing things away,
I 'm joining my school eco committee to give ideas to help save the world,
E very person can do something to help,
N ever give up and always keep going with your dreams to save the world,
D own the trees go, why are we doing this?
L ater on, there might not even be a world, so let's change now,
Y ou're the person who can change it, come on.

Nathan Whooley (9)
Willington School, Wimbledon

The Snow Leopard

S ave the rare creatures before they disappear,
N ever let them leave our world,
O r we will shed a tear.
W e only have a few thousand left.

L et them live a peaceful life,
E arth wouldn't be the same without them.
O n the snow, hunters kill them with a knife,
P rotect these precious animals before it's too late.
A s we let them be, they will grow in number,
R unning wild, they will have a happy existence,
D on't delay because we can do this together!

Ben Cryer (8)
Willington School, Wimbledon

The Green Planet

G o! Go! Go, global citizens,
R oar! The graceful wildlife roars out our name,
E very day trying to save our planet,
E nvironmental planet, think of that,
N o more deforestation,

P eople of Earth, sustain our wonderful home,
L ife is amazing, join our song,
A ct now for the planet and for our lives,
N ever ever forget, think green planet,
E vergreen forests must grow and grow,
T hink of the planet all day long.

Tom Castle (10)
Willington School, Wimbledon

The Midnight Fox

The midnight fox looks at the night sky,
He hears the creatures scurrying around,
But the midnight fox is very shy,
So he lies on the ground,
And looks to the things that fly.

There are many creatures that fly,
Such as bats with black wings,
Butterflies with wings that go high,
And flying squirrels that fling.

There are also creatures down below,
Like moles that dig in the soil,
Snails that go slow,
Bugs that steadily coil.

So now you know,
What fox sees,
What's up in the sky,
And down deep below.

Orlando Othoro (10)
Willington School, Wimbledon

Komodo Dragon

K omodo dragons
O ccasionally enjoy a shoreline dip
M ost are venomous
O pen grassland is where they are found
D ragon-like lizard
O nly 4000 left in our world

D oesn't fly or breathe out fire
R ising sea level's a danger to them
A lmost any meat they eat
G rowing up to 10 feet long and weighing 150 pounds
O r more
N ot to be a pet, better wild and free.

Christian Stephenson Macharia (7)
Willington School, Wimbledon

Pollution Based On Victorians

A misty morning, 12:00 on the dot,
I tried to look for my penny to go to school,
In no hope, I walked to school, knowing I would be beaten by annoying Miss Eileen,
In fear, I put my head up to see the pollution this disgraceful country has,
The sky is grey as gloom, as grim as the Plague, 150 years later:
Now in 2003, we all realize this cost and what this has done to affect us,
The moral of the story is to be respectful to the Earth,
Like how we want to be treated, this is our living.

Sam Bemana (9)
Willington School, Wimbledon

Leaves

Leaves are the fantastic things on trees,
Green, red, brown, and yellow,
All their own special colour,
When the breeze breathes its gentle breath,
The leaves flutter their small wings.

They come in a variety of shapes, colours, and sizes,
They may be helicopter-like, spinning in the wind,
Or they might be needle-sharp, piercing clothes,
Or even broad and giant.

They cover the floor of the woods,
Making a blissful bed for birds,
They come to the end of their lives,
Rotting away there.

Charlie Nailon
Willington School, Wimbledon

What Am I?

Dressed in shirts of black and gold,
I work very hard, busy and bold.

Working in a team and collecting nectar as I go,
I fly over fields and gardens, searching for flowers below.

Don't worry about my sting, it doesn't mean a thing!
I'm actually very good, but I'm just misunderstood.

My mission is to pollinate so we can all thrive.
Without me and my buzzing buddies, we will not survive.

Fin Pittam (7)
Willington School, Wimbledon

Glaciers

G lobal warming is a problem,
L eaders aren't doing anything to change,
A ction has to be taken by the public,
C hildren today can make a difference,
I deas to stop this problem are welcome,
E veryone can change the way we live,
R espect for our planet is vitally important,
S top the melting of our glaciers.

Elias Carle-Edgar (9)
Willington School, Wimbledon

Australian Wildfire Horror

Far away from the cold, icy UK, you get the beautiful Aussie outback,
But the forest is the sun, smacked down into the world,
The fires leave the wildlife-packed forest a black, sooty, orange wasteland,
Many animals have to be rescued, but many remain to burn to a boney crisp,
Just looking at the stunning forest go black with soot makes everyone cry with sadness and shame.

Marcus Kipps (9)
Willington School, Wimbledon

Can You Help?

The blue planet,
Do you care?
The climate is changing,
Can you help?
The ice caps are shrinking,
Polar bears cry,
Will you waste less?
And stop your car,
The oceans have plastic,
And turtles die,
Can you plant trees,
So we can survive?

Ben Nestor (7)
Willington School, Wimbledon

Save The Tigers

T igers prowl in the jungle,
I n search of their prey,
G iant leaps across the jungle,
E ndangered creatures need protecting,
R oaring loudly, as loud as thunder,
S ave tigers, they are amazing!

Henry Uden (7)
Willington School, Wimbledon

Apple

A seed is planted;
A tree shall grow.
The tree shall be big and tall,
And sprout its buds,
Then in the summer,
The buds grow,
And turn into an apple.
Someone will eat the
Apple,
Then plant the seed.
The cycle of the apple
Is everlasting.

George Cant (10)
Willington School, Wimbledon

Poor Polar Bear

A polar bear is cuddly,
A polar bear is bubbly,
He is sad because he has nothing to eat,
He has no ice to support his feet,
Global warming has ruined his life,
He has no children or polar bear wife.

Matthew Cox (8)
Willington School, Wimbledon

Save The Pandas

P andas are in danger,
A s numbers are low,
N aughty people have
D amaged the environment,
A nd now we shall protect them.

Oscar Cormack (7)
Willington School, Wimbledon

The Earth

I am a sphere,
I am what you are standing on,
I have a sparkle of blue and a touch of green,
I have a very bright moon,
Save our planet!

Charlie Thomas (7)
Willington School, Wimbledon

Talking Nature

I like woodpeckers pecking on the tree,
I like bees that live in me,
I like trees swishing and swashing,
I like the wind bishing and bashing.

Thomas Massy (7)
Willington School, Wimbledon

Deforestation Haikus

Where trees have been felled,
And habitats demolished,
Animals will die.

Humans must restore
Foliage, plants and forests,
To end this problem.

William Booth (11)
Willington School, Wimbledon

YOUNG WRITERS INFORMATION

We hope you have enjoyed reading this book – and that you will continue to in the coming years.

If you're the parent or family member of an enthusiastic poet or story writer, do visit our website **www.youngwriters.co.uk/subscribe** and sign up to receive news, competitions, writing challenges and tips, activities and much, much more! There's lots to keep budding writers motivated!

If you would like to order further copies of this book, or any of our other titles, then please give us a call or order via your online account.

Young Writers
Remus House
Coltsfoot Drive
Peterborough
PE2 9BF
(01733) 890066
info@youngwriters.co.uk

Join in the conversation!
Tips, news, giveaways and much more!

YoungWritersUK   YoungWritersCW   youngwriterscw

Scan me to watch The Big Green video!